The Mind and Heart

martha agius

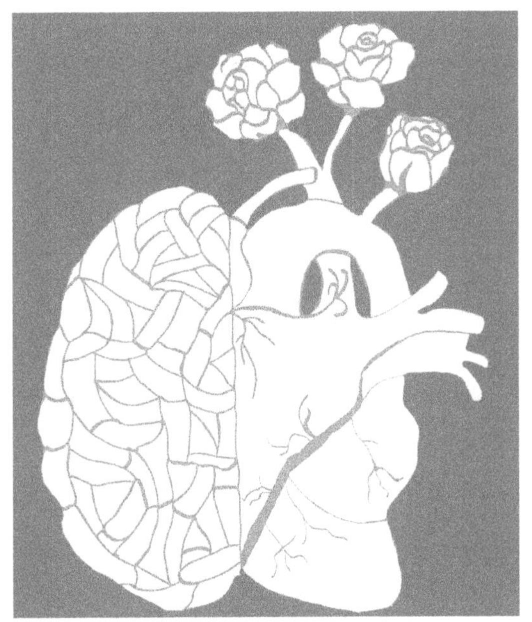

Acknowledgements

I would like to thank the following people: Ms Maria Cutajar for being the first to believe in me, Mrs Sarah Abela for encouraging me to publish my work, Mrs Diana Carabott for mentoring and proofreading the poetry and Mrs Dorienne Grech, Ms Leanne Lewis and Mr Keith Balzan for editing, typesetting and designing the collection. I am grateful to Mr Joseph Ellul, head of school at SMC Verdala, for his help and continuous support, along with the Vittoriosa Local Council and BDL Publishers for believing in my work. Thanks goes as well to my friends and family, especially Isaac, for their love and encouragement. If it had not been for these people this collection of poetry would not have been possible.

First published in Malta in 2020
by St Margaret College Secondary School Verdala
and funded by Vittoriosa Local Council
www.smcsecondary.com

ISBN: 978-99957-1-702-5

Illustrations and book cover by martha agius
Typeset and Design by D. Grech, L. Lewis & K. Balzan
Printed by Book Distributors Limited

The Mind and Heart

To my sister,

Though I never had the chance
To witness your face,
In my heart you've always
Held a special place.

The Mind and Heart

my mind is an overthinker
it ties me down.

but my heart
is fiercer
my mind
tells me one thing
but my heart
dances to a different ring.

to whom should i listen?
do i follow my heart
and its ambition?
or my mind
and its prison?

to whom should i listen
to my heart
and its precisions
or my mind
and its decisions?

I've Lost Myself

i've lost the person i once was
Come to think it was all because:

a sharpened blade against my skin
a devilish face with a malicious grin,
a mind that never stops to overthink
a person who thought i was just a thing,
a mouth that never wanted to open
a friend that promised he'll never stop hoping,
a bully that pummeled me with words
a friend who stabbed me in the back with swords,

a heart that ended up as stone
a soul that always felt alone.

Thou Made My Heart Ache

my heart aches,
there's so much
i've lost
for thy sake.

like an army in a war
has its alliance
thou attacked me
till i had no self-defiance.

like a hunter shoots
his next prey
like them thou left me
on the ground to lay.

That Moment

i keep going back to that moment
when you took my heart
when life felt perfect
until it all fell apart.

if i could go back to that moment
i'd erase you from my mind,
i would run away from you
and leave you there behind.

if i could take you back to that moment
to make you feel what i felt
for you to understand
with what i had dealt.

…and maybe then you could see
what it feels to be me.

Messed Up

how would i have known
all the lies he had sworn
were to build his throne,
all the hate he had shown
reflected his own
feelings of being left alone

a broken boy
victim of his own mind.

Back To You

i wish to forget all the things i've been through
all the time i wasted looking back at you,
i don't want to, i never had
but the thoughts in my mind have fled.

why did you do it? it's all i want to know.
you showed no care, no care to hear no
i gave you my trust still you chose to break me.
you tried to control me.

no is a simple word, why couldn't you hear?
you showed no mercy not even when i broke into tears
all i felt towards you was fear, nothing more
i couldn't move, nor speak, and right there my world
turned bleak,

i wish to forget all the things i've been through
i want to go back and hit rewind to feel brand new,
i know i can't change it but why can't i forget
can't i just ignore it and act as if we never met?

Your Decision

she was once a girl you admired
that one kiss from her you desired,
but when she was yours
you shut her down closing your own doors.

now she's with someone new
you've thrown away all of what you've been through,
for another girl who you thought could give you
much more than her,
but when things got serious that girl
bolted and then you knew,
that she had been the one for you.

Can You Realize

can you realize what you've done?
the words as your bullets
and your mouth the fired gun
and as you spoke
her you broke.

if she could, she would ask
why wear such a dull mask?
are you contempt?
in turning her to a bird
captured in a net?

Stung By A Jellyfish

it wrapped its tentacles
around my neck
Stinging and burning,
i felt dead
i ripped it off
i was a wreck.

you burn and destroy
i screamed but you enjoy.

at least now you know
the reason you'll end up alone,
is because you use and throw
a jellyfish hiding behind a stone.

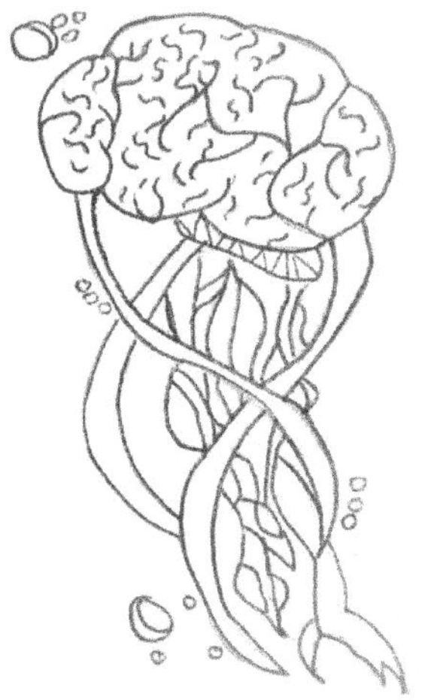

Left Me Alone

why did you leave me
right here all alone?
with the person i feared
that i once have known.

why did you leave me?
when you could have stayed
i wish you'd believe me
but inside me i prayed.

why did you leave me?
with the monster i am,
thoughts that feed on me
to be free, i never can.

why did you leave me
right when i was alright?
then you left me behind
left my old emotions
that had burnt me
to once again re-ignite

Tied Up

do you ever feel tied up within?
like a knot inside
that you just cannot get rid of it?

try to calm down and breathe in
but the feeling
you just can get rid of it.

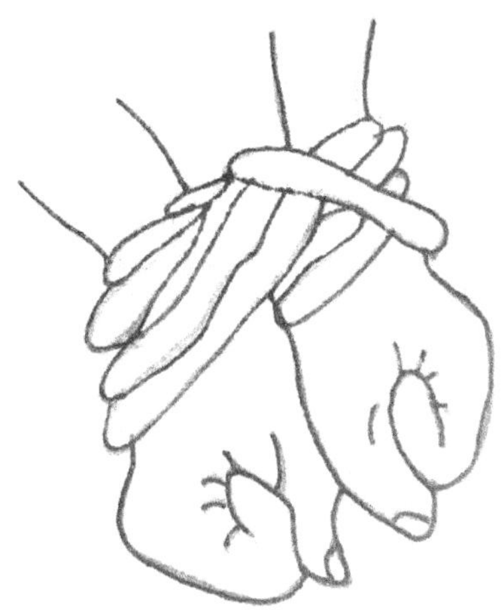

Dynasty

i built a dynasty
for us,
a place of fantasy
and love.

you had the reign,
all ours
a place with no pain
just us.

if only that was enough,
just me,
but i was the only one in love
with us.

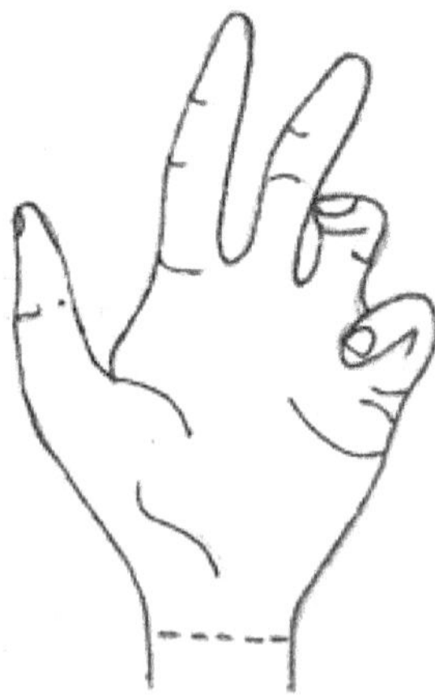

Am I The Tool?

am i a tool
in a box of nuts and bolts
am i the fool
to allow you
to be so cruel?

A Girl Gone Wrong

the heart, it was beating
but her pulse was numb
her innocence she defeated
when she lost herself to rum.

she chose to escape from sorrow
to run from her past mistakes
chose to live like there's no tomorrow
becoming a person, she hates.

Sins And Innocence
21

drowning away
in pools of sins,
forgetting the girl
who was washed
in waterfalls
of innocence.

she could not believe
what she had become
and could not remember
the song that she sung.

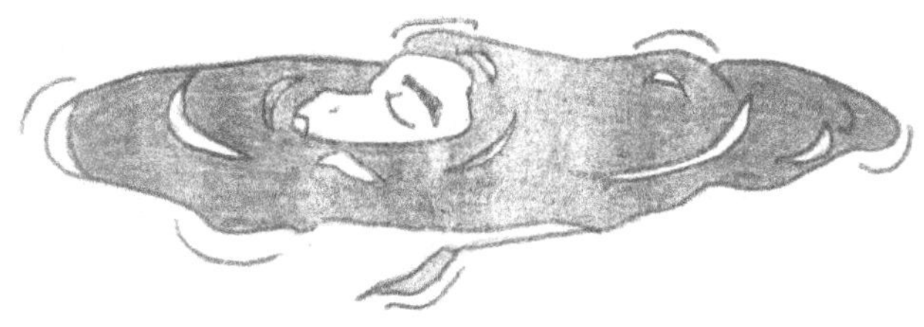

On The Surface

beneath the thick skin
that you see when you pass by
there is a broken heart buried within
come close, you will see how thin.

i am not so tough
as i seem to be,
but life was rough
it took a toll on me

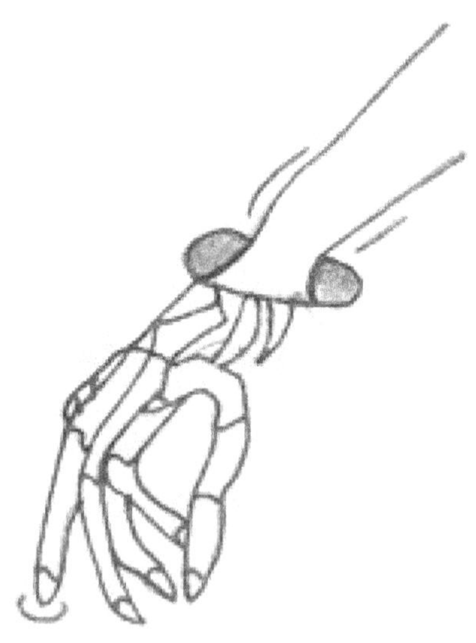

In Your Skin

we have been here before
do you remember it all?
you wonder why
this happens all the time.

you try so hard
just to fit in
repeating situations,
then you begin.

what did i do wrong?
you think to yourself
they think you're so strong
but you're breaking
real thin.

you say you belong
some other place but here,
but how can you go?
when you don't belong
in your own skin.

Silence Too Loud

your silence is too loud
can you hear it?
emptiness within your mouth
can you hear it?

your silence
drove me deaf
your breathing
is all i have left.

speak up and be quiet
leave peace in me
put your fears aside
your mouth is not the trap
but the key to be free.

As I'm Silent

please hear me out
even though my mouth
leaves no trace,
make up the words
from a look at my face.

How I wish

how i wish
i had the skin
that glows
and sun kissed,

how i wish
i was the person
that you miss.

I've Hurt Him

i have shattered him
to pieces
as small as mine
that i was
cracked so fine
that i cut him
too.

my eyes saw him
but my mind
refused to see,
that it wasn't him
who broke me
but the one
who helped
to unfold me.

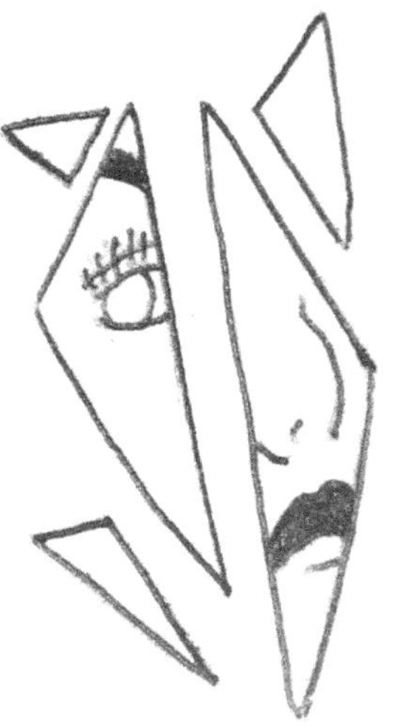

In My Sleep

i am talking in my sleep
some nights
i can't even sleep,
i have passed the age
where i can count
my black and white sheep.

i try to close my eyes
but the ones
that i despise
come out to
tell their own
truthful lies.

now it's 3am
i still look around
trying to figure out
why i feel so lost
and i ask myself,

when will i be found?

Midnight

when the sun turns down the light
and hides from the sky
the light falls on into the night
the pain starts showing in her eye.

when the rain decides to fall onto her face
and the feeling of his touch
is nothing but a cold embrace.

Mending

why is it so hard?
to believe what you say
pretending as though so smart
i try to put my thoughts to lay.

can you listen to my mind
when it shouts out to you
do you pretend to be blind?
just because it's nothing new.

can we talk this time
instead of pretending,
is it ok if I'm not fine
can i tell you my heart is still mending?

Heal

i put the pieces back to their place
i couldn't fill all the missing space
but slowly by new pieces them i'll replace.

i try to stitch my open scars
of self-inflicted wounds of harm
but as i threaded lightly the needle broke
so i wrapped it up and hoped it would hold.

Surrender

i give my heart time to heal
from all the hurt it feels,
i myself have chosen to surrender
so once again i can defend her.

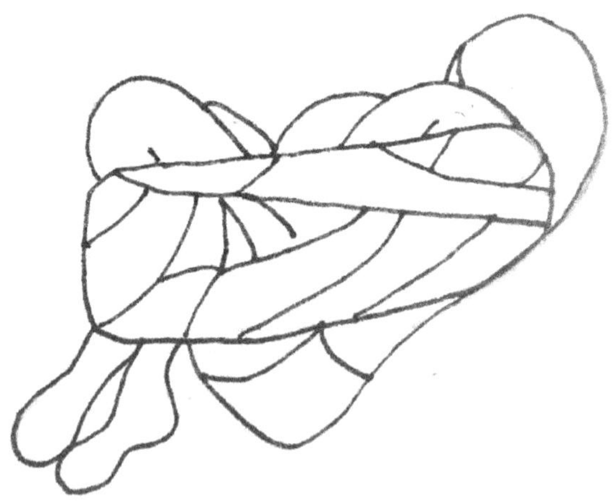

Strip Away

as today i take
my body at hand
and strip away
the label and brand,
how i do hope
to find
the person i am inside.

From Now On

from now on
i'll focus on being a daisy,
from now on i won't wish
to be a rose,
let my life no longer be hazy
may i no longer appose.

My soul

i'm beautifully made
i will realize
Once my face has
Faded.
then i'd know
that my body
isn't as important
as my soul.

it doesn't matter
What size or colour
But,
the kindness in your heart
embracing that life is your art
finally, now you can
face it
finally, now you can
embrace it.

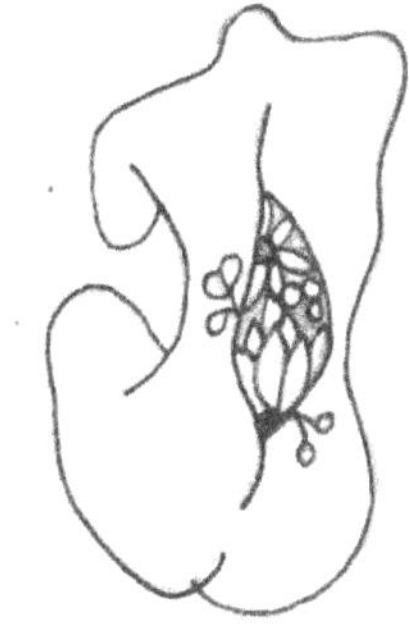

Move On

if you'd ask me
what i want from life,
i'd say i beg for no goodbyes,
i'd ask you to hold me at night
and stop my heart
from aching inside.

but i know now that that's not right
i need to move on
to wipe you from my heart
and learn to carry on.

Not Mine To Control

if tomorrow i wake up blue
where the wheels have turned
and once again i think of you,

shall i no longer ponder
why you did the things you've done
may i no longer wonder
why my heart became undone,

then a new day will rise
and your face well be a haze
i will no longer hear truth
when the words are all lies
and finally, i will realize
that you were just a phase.

I've Fallen

it runs through my veins
courses through my blood,
picture perfect hung in frames
a type of love my heart has flood.

he gives me strength,
he gave me power
he gave me water
for my seed to turn to a flower,
i never could've known
that from the first time we kissed
that if i never had met him,
a part of me i would've missed.

Ecstasy

ecstasy in your arms
my strongest longing,
feeling out of all harm
an all-time feeling
from night to morning,
convincing by charm,
a free fall, i'm soaring
though if i fall
you'll hold me through it all.

Lay Down By Me

lay by me
tell me it's ok,
right beside me
forever you will stay.

i'm not an easy person
this i'll admit,
but don't push me away
please don't forbid.

i can be distant
most of the time,
don't give up
just tell me we're fine.

i have trust issues
quite a lot,
but i opened up to you
to you i come forth.

Stronger Now

i'm stronger 'cause you taught
me to be one
you told me how things
should be done,
you taught me not to run
all my messes have
been undone
even though i had a ton
but now my life has begun.

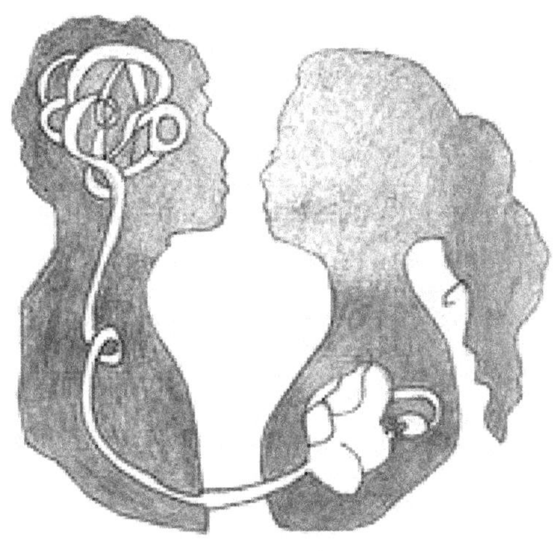

Afraid to lose

i want to go back to the day we first met
to feel the things that we once felt,
for love seemed easy, when you held my hand
when love was simple, beautiful and grand.

though i doubt my love will fade
my worst nightmare is to be betrayed,
to you the future i cannot promise
i'm not perfect, i am no goddess.

to you, my love i'd give
my mistakes i wish you to forgive,
i hope i will never do you no harm
although i'm scared, for you i'll disarm.

i'm jealous for all the hands you've touched
because i never loved someone as much,
i can't stand to see you with another
because if i let you go
my heart will never recover.

Together

don't tell me you need a break
please don't let my heart flake
don't tell me you need time
please don't tell me
you're not mine
i can't pretend
to be fine,

if you need to change
we can change together
if you need to grow
we can grow as we go.

Do I Love You?

est-ce que je t'aime?
je pense que je t'aime
do i love you?
i think i do.

to love another person
don't i have to love myself?
i have to be a better version
but will i ever except myself?

am i enough? i ask all the time
but i refuse to lose you
i know one day i will be fine
but i have to have you by my side.

will you stay, now that you know
that my biggest bully is me,
but i know i can be worthy although
i'm not worthy to me.

First Lover

burning like fire in the flames
someone free me from these chains
i'm locked up by my own fault
by the bullet, by that bolt,

i lived like this all my life
against my skin a hateful knife
they asked and i said i was fine
but i was living a life that wasn't mine.

i chose to take it back
self-love i wouldn't lack
for if i'm to love another
i have to put myself as my first lover.

To Love A Sunflower

a sunflower and a rose
they are both pretty,
but the rose is the queen bee.

it is unsettling, what a pity
that people prefer to pick up a rose
because it represents love and beauty,

but if it symbolizes love why does it hurt?
why do we allow such self-cruelty?

Who am I?

i'm made up of continuous mistakes
most of my choices i wish to replace,
i lose my patience quite a lot
until i realize what i've got,
i'm not my body neither my height
i'm not what you see within your sight,
don't judge me from what you see
get to know me then either shoes to stay
Or choose to flee.

Different Worlds

we live on the same earth
but stand on different worlds
its not the place we're in
but the experience of pain and hurt.

not the oceans surrounding us
nor the mountains over our head
nor the grass beneath our feet
nor the clouds rain and suns heat

but the love between two
moments shared with them and you.

Waves Of Emotions

life is full of waves
not just oceans,
the way we behave
and our emotions,
they come and go
the highs and lows,
but all we know
is a constant flow
of good and bad
all the moments we had.

Daydreamer,

The drilling doubts drag my feet to go to places that my mind does not know, while my body roams around, my mind is left to act as if it was already found. A world I built awaits me. Any second I have I daydream, to escape from the dreaded world, to go back to creatures from my childhood I miss. I lose myself and don't even notice an hour has passed, but I've lost my focus, for an hour I went to a place I was sent, it might not be real but it's better than anything else.

Bright Side

look at the bright side
you woke up today,
to lovebirds chirping
you put your troubles away
you roll out of bed, hoping
open your window to sunlight beams
your eyes ache to the thought
of never achieving your dreams,
just as they ache with the day's dusk.

you put on the same pair of jeans
from the day before,
put your hair in a messed-up bun
your feet drill the floor just trying,
to get out of your bedroom door.

but tomorrow try to
get up from bed, shake it all off
open the window, look outside and adore,
embrace the birds chirping
and be grateful for it all.

Forever Young

can we stay forever young?
with these highs that fill my lungs
can the night refrain from lasting?
as to these moments
i find myself grasping.

may i never say goodbye
to these flames that ignite,
with the burning sun
in a summer flashing light.

Beautiful Summer

pretty skies
and warm yellow,
messy hair
and water's shallow.

glorious nights
a beautiful breeze,
marvelous sights
that never seize.

all of this reminds me of you
please come back to me
oh! beautiful summer.

If only I could say

if only i could say
that i laid on the ground
waiting to be found
by you someday
like a flower awaits to bloom
or the stars to find the moon
i'd hope you'll find me soon.

...and then i can say that i've bloomed too

I'm Found

my life has been a bit though
but it's what i needed to learn i'm enough.

a family that loves me stood by my side
a thought after everything i still tried,
a heart that finally broke through its wall
a mind that stopped thinking of it all,

i've realized that

i've been given this life for a reason
to live throughout the seasons,
and now i'm able to see
that i have to learn to just be me.

Sorry for running away

i'm sorry i came out
too strong
it's just that 've never
felt i belong
i get attached
but quickly move along
but i do so because I fear
that my intuition was wrong
i like you
i always will
maybe i was scared
maybe i'm still,
did you like me?
was i right to run
or was i blind to see?
maybe all i wanted was a friend
who cares
and will be there till the end,
but is it too late?
have i lost you?
i'll leave it up to faith
maybe i'll come
back again to you.

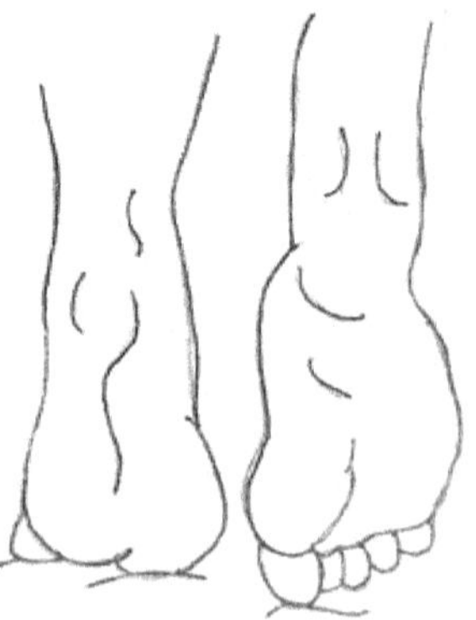

About the author

Martha Agius is a 16 year old Maltese student. She developed a love for poetry at a very young and later on was inspired by other writers and was encouraged to pursue a career in writing. Most of her inspiration lies in everyday experiences and she feels that poetry offers the creative release she and others need.

Instagram: @martha_agius

Website: poetryisartistic.com